CHOSEN
FOR THE
CHALLENGE

Faith, Miracles &
How We Overcome
Our Greatest Challenges

Apostle Mark A. Hatcher, Sr.

Copyright © 2022 Mark A. Hatcher, Sr.

All rights reserved. No part of this book may be reproduced in any form or by any electronic or mechanical means, including information storage and retrieval systems, without permission in writing from the publisher, except by reviewers, who may quote brief passages in a review.

ISBN: 978-1-955312-44-8

Printed in the United States of America
Story Corner Publishing & Consulting, Inc.
1510 Atlanta Ave.
Portsmouth, VA 23704

Storycornerpublishing@yahoo.com
www.StoryCornerPublishing.com

Dedication

God blessed me with a spiritual father, Morris Cerullo, to carry me throughout ministry and give me the tools to be a servant and a leader. Papa Cerullo has imparted into me the gift of prophecy to the nations, faith, wisdom, knowledge, and most of all, the agape love for God's people. The countless hours of ministry that I have spent serving this giant and the body of Christ will forever be treasured and remembered. I thank God for the legacy center and the life of my spiritual father, Papa Cerullo. I dedicate this book to him. ~Mark A. Hatcher Sr.

Morris and Theresa Cerullo

Fond memories with Dr. Morris and Theresa Cerullo

I remember this day. It was like a father and son day. We had fun with the milkshakes and took in a relaxation time. It was a great day to be with my spiritual parents. We took the pictures along the side were taken on another one of our fun times in New York. The Cerrullo's always loved traveling, enjoying good connections and good food.

Foreword

I am more than honored to write the foreword for a God-fearing man who is powerful and yet extremely humble. From the first time I met Apostle Mark A. Hatcher Sr., his countenance was one of a calm and welcoming spirit. When I began to learn more about his story, I could see how God had placed him where he is for such a time as this. As I sat with Apostle Hatcher and began to conceive his concept for the book, it took me into the world of the true warrior's journey, one that comes from the most genuine heart of a God worshipper and a faithful follower of Christ. ~Joy Linn Mackey

Table of Contents

Preface ix

The MET 1910 2

Chronology Of Use 3

Biographical Sketch 4

Chapter 1 Beginnings: Little Things Mean a Lot 7

Chapter 2 Childhood: We Are Overcomers 11

Chapter 3 Prayer Life: Prayer, Prayer & More Prayer 17

Chapter 4 The Road: When the Road Is Rough
 and The Going Gets Tough 23

Chapter 5 Camp Meeting 31

Chapter 6 Life is a Journey 43

Chapter 7 Renovated Met 47

Chapter 8 Blast from the Past 53

Chapter 9 Great Moments 67

Chapter 10 Ribbon Cutting 71

Chapter 11 MET Photos & News Clips 75

Chapter 12 Ending Segment 83

Preface

It was essential for me to write this book. It has been over 30 years of pouring into destiny and the call to do what God has required. I want to go even deeper to help others realize that I am not the only chosen one. I want people to realize that they are also chosen for an assignment, and now is the time to awaken to it. I want to continue to inspire people to believe in God and believe in themselves.

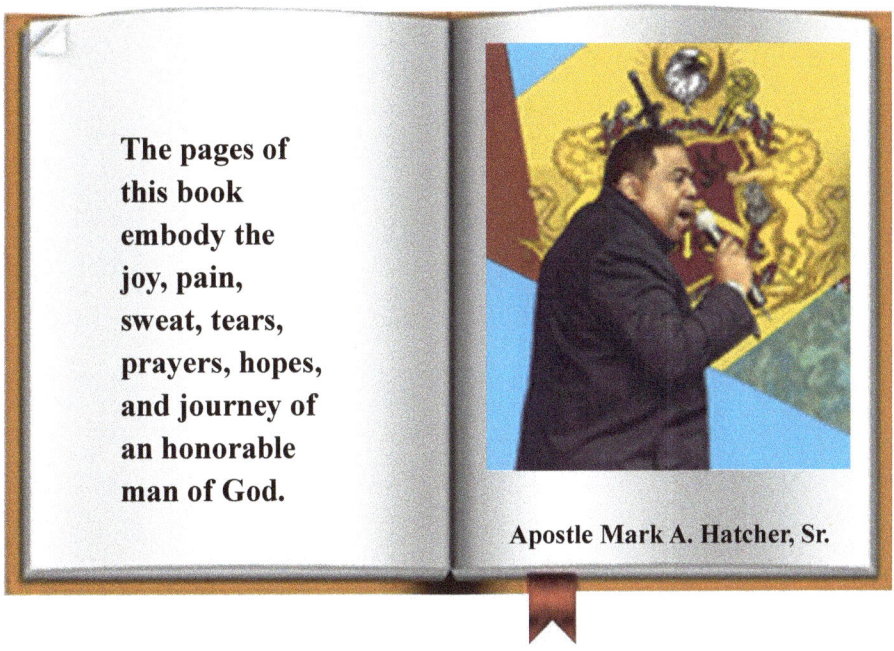

The pages of this book embody the joy, pain, sweat, tears, prayers, hopes, and journey of an honorable man of God.

Apostle Mark A. Hatcher, Sr.

"And your people will rebuild the ancient ruins; You will raise up and restore the age-old foundations [of buildings that have been laid waste]; You will be called Repairer of the Breach, Restorer of Streets with Dwellings."
~Isaiah 58:12 NIV

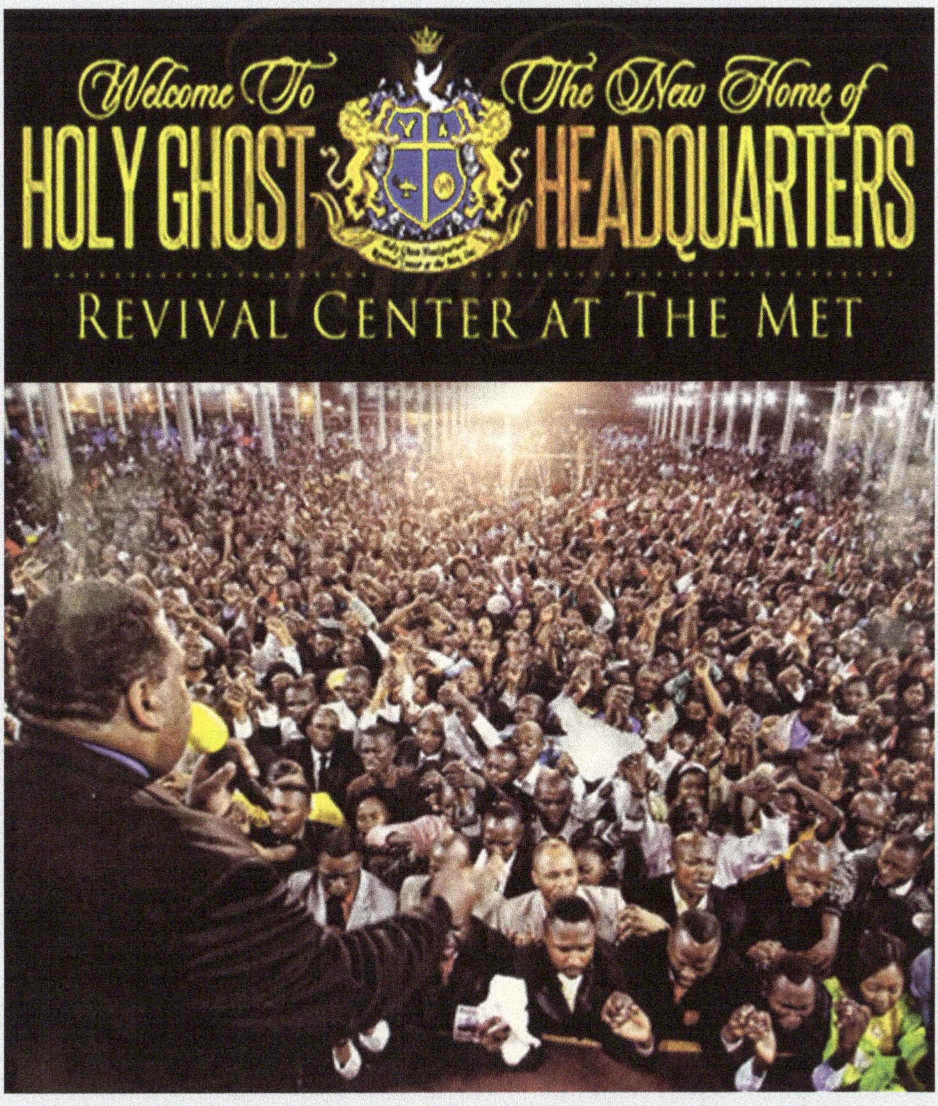

Apostle Mark A. Hatcher Sr.

WORLDWIDE FAITH MINISTRIES

The MET 1910

There are quite a few stories about this striking architectural monument called "The MET." In this picture, she stands with great prestige. She was not the first grand theater in our fair city. Broadway lyricist Oscar Hammerstein opened the Philadelphia Opera House to rival the Academy of Music in 1908. However, he found himself weighed down in debt and forced to sell to his rival, who named the building the Metropolitan Opera House, or what Philadelphians call it, "The Met." My story with the MET, including the juicy trimmings, is located on each page.

Chronology of Use
Metropolitan Opera House (The Met)
(Also known as The Philadelphia Opera House (1908-1929), the Philadelphia Evangelistic Center 1953-1989, and currently The Holy Ghost Headquarters Revival Center at The Met 1996-Present)

Construction completed in 1908 (Commissioned by Opera Promoter, Oscar Hammerstein-Architect William H, McElfatrick (1854-1922)

Hammerstein sold the building in 1910 to Edward T. Stotesbury for $1.2 million (Hammerstein experienced financial trouble due to low attendance at performances.)

Stotesbury sold the building to Knights of the Mystic Shrine in 1920. The building was used for vaudeville, legitimate theatre, and some opera.

The building was sold to Stanley Corporation in 1928. It was used for a movie theatre-renamed The Met.

Sports promoter Jimmy Toppi acquires the building from 1939-1954. He used it for boxing, wrestling, and basketball events.

Dr. Thea F. Jones preached at The Met in 1953 and acquired building in 1955. From 1953 through 1988, the building was known as the Philadelphia Evangelistic Center at the Met (Also known as The Met Church.) (Dr. Jones completed many repairs and acquired historic certification for building from 1970 through 1972 (on City, State, and National Historic Registers.)

Apostle Mark Hatcher, a congregant of Dr. Jones, acquired the building in 1996. It is known as The Holy Ghost Headquarters Revival Center at The Met.

Source: Konick Architectural Firm 2006

Biographical Sketch of
Apostle Mark Hatcher, Sr., D.D.

Apostle Mark A. Hatcher, son of the late Robert Hatcher and Therenthia Hatcher, was born and raised in the heart of North Philadelphia. He was educated in the Philadelphia Public School System and graduated from Simon Gratz High School. His family was devoted members of the Met Church under the tutelage of the late Dr. Thea F. Jones. At an early age, Mark Hatcher converted to Christianity and displayed a love for witnessing to others with and beyond his years. His desire to encourage people to heed the invitation to accept the Lord Jesus Christ was seemingly unquenchable. As a teenager, Mark Hatcher was obedient to the call from God to the ministry and was appointed Associate Pastor of the MET Church in 1981.

Mark Hatcher established the Mark Hatcher Evangelistic Crusades in 1983 and became the Pastor of the Holy Ghost Headquarters Church in the same year. The church was located in a dilapidated building in North Philadelphia and required renovations before it became a sanctuary of refuge for a rapidly expanding congregation.

In 1995 God gave Apostle Hatcher a vision to restore the MET. The registered historic building located at Broad & Poplar Streets was scheduled for demolition. Still, Apostle Hatcher was commissioned to restore the facility and contribute to the community's revitalization. The undertaking would be monumental and would require massive funding and unwavering faith. When it comes to faith, believing, pronouncing, and experiencing the promises of God, Apostle Hatcher is full of faith. With the backing of the congregation, funding was pouring in, and great work was in progress

Brief List of Accomplishments

- ❖ Voice of the Spirit Radio Broadcast
- ❖ Voice of the Spirit Television Broadcast
- ❖ Pray for the City Prayer Vigil
- ❖ Food Distribution Program for the Needy

- Outreach Ministry – Street Evangelism
- Renaissance in Recovery Rehab
- Morris Cerullo School of Ministry – Philly
- International Evangelist – Preached in Asia, Africa, Europe, and South America

Apostle Hatcher has made positive impressions within the North Philadelphia community. He is a product of the North Philadelphia community, and he has the determination to see a positive change.

Apostle Hatcher's family worshiped at The Met under the pastoral leadership of the late Dr. Thea Jones (1920-1992), founder of the Evangelistic Crusades and the Philadelphia Evangelistic Center at the Met from 1955 until 1984. The congregation was, during this period, unusual in its interracial composition. During Rev. Jones's tenure at the Met, his healing and worship services drew more than 5,000 people. As a young person, Hatcher had a passion and love for witnessing for the Lord. Apostle Hatcher was ordained to the ministry as a teenager, and in 1983 established the Hatcher Evangelical Center in North Philadelphia.

In 1993, Rev. Jones, widow, Helen Jones, contacted Apostle Hatcher to assist with saving the Met, which had fallen into disrepair following Rev. Jones' death. The courts had ordered the demolition of the building within 30 days. Apostle Hatcher established Holy Ghost Headquarters Revival Center at the Met in 1994. Ownership of the building was transferred to Apostle Hatcher after he met the court requirements to halt the demolition of the building. God gave Apostle Hatcher the vision to rescue the building and blessed him with the support of his congregation, his spiritual father, Rev. Morris Cerullo, and other national clergy leaders to stabilize the building for approximately 20 years.

In 2013 negotiations were held with the historic developer of the Divine Lorraine Hotel, Eric Blumenfeld. In 2016, a collaborative agreement was struck with Blumenfeld, which culminated in a complete $56 million-dollar restoration of this historically registered building. Apostle Hatcher notes that "the building restoration is a fulfillment of the vision given to me by God. The Met will not only house the worship and other services of the church but will also provide the community with needed services and support. After 22 years of holding on, despite skeptics, our prayers and fasting have been answered through our faith in God."

Apostle Hatcher has a doctorate in Divinity from the Divinity Grace Theological Seminary. He is a member of the Philadelphia Council of Clergy. His ministry is both local and global as he travels extensively with crusades.

Chapter 1

Beginnings: Little Things Mean a Lot

Of all the things Christ wants for us, loving him and focusing our attention on him are the most important. ~ Charles Stanley

There is a point and time when something starts. It is called the origination, the birth, the dawn, or the genesis. Scripture beckons us not to despise these small things because God loves to see us carry out his work.

- ❖ An acorn starts small
- ❖ A mustard seed starts small
- ❖ A rosebud starts small
- ❖ Greatness starts small

In 1983 I started evangelizing at Majestic Temple under my pastor Rev. Anthony Floyd, hosting weekend services. I never aspired to be a pastor, I saw the things pastors went through, and as far as I was concerned, evangelism was more my thing. My goal was to evangelize on the weekends.

But over time, I started realizing that many people did not have a church, and that is when I began to pastor. Growing up in the MET as a youth, I became the youngest youth pastor there. I also worked there mopping floors. Eventually, to my surprise, I became manager at the MET. I began to sense that the Lord had me in a place of training and serving. I could see that it was a place for God to prepare me. I could not become a great pastor without having the experience of serving.

In 1995 the MET was preparing to close its doors. My pastor was getting older, and I was on my journey, not realizing that God had released me from there to prepare me to come back to the MET a little while later. Therefore, I say I was Chosen for the Challenge.

I spent seven years in a rented building at Broad and Green Streets and then another seven years in a rented building at 13th & Clearfield Street. During this time, I was learning the construction business. Around the same time, I started to have genuine empathy and compassion for a group of men that lived in a rehab in Altoona, Pennsylvania. For five years, I would drive four hours to Altoona, in the snow, in the rain, you name it. I would preach an eight o'clock pm service and then drive four hours back home.

My mindset said I dare not stop, we were building men up spiritually, and there were many men in that house. I was blessed to meet a friend who had a gift for carpentry, and without realizing it, I found that there were many skilled men in that house. And just like that, destiny arrived. This man's gifts allowed the work to begin in the house. Within thirty days, we had stabilized the interior part of the building. This man's gifts made room for not only him but for others.

Everyone is born with a gift.

- A Gift to Serve
- A Gift for Public Speaking
- A Gift of Wisdom
- A Gift for Building
- A Gift of Writing
- A Gift for Teaching
- A Gift for Networking
- A Gift of Faith
- A Gift of Leadership
- A Gift of Mercy

What are your gifts? Are you using your gifts? Remember, your gifts make room for you.

Chapter 2

Childhood:
We Are Overcomers

The great people of the earth today are the people who pray, (not) those who talk about prayer. ~ S.D. Gordon

I was in the Get Set program at Thankful Baptist Church when I was four years old. Get Set is mostly about getting children ready for the experiences they will need along the way. The teachers were nice. We did a lot of running, skipping, puzzles, blocks, finger painting, and drawing. But right in the middle of it all, at four years old, I fell backward and injured my lower back and spine.

Therefore, I had to have operations on my back at St. Christopher's Hospital. Sometimes I would cry uncontrollable and inconsolable tears when my family members had to leave the hospital. It was like a dark night of the soul. But I consoled myself because I knew they were just as sad as I was to have me there alone. All I can say is that I am grateful because the fall could have paralyzed me, but hallelujah, God had another idea.

One of the things I am dearly grateful for is having the father that I had. I know he loved me. There was no doubt. I was his pride and joy. I loved my mother and siblings so much, but the times I spent with my dad was unforgettable.

At six years old, I was standing on a tin bucket I called my pulpit, and I would evangelize to people. I even went into the bar and asked people if they needed prayer. I knew it would agitate some people, but they were always kind enough to realize that I was doing God's work. And many times, they would give me a quarter to get out so that they could go back to what they called fun.

I also went to the store for people. There is nothing wrong with doing good deeds. As far as I see it, there is everything right about it. And that is why I would be sure to let them know that I was praying for them. Even things like going to the barbershop turned into another one of my opportunities to shine the light of Christ.

Some of my fond memories were when my father would take me with him as he gave communion to the sick or shut-in. My dad was a great man. I also remember the time he took me down south with him. I was nine years old. My dad's old house was in Georgia. He walked into the old house he grew up in, and I saw him looking around and reminiscing on the property. He must have realized his life was coming to an end.

When we came back from Georgia, my dad had surgery. I remember in fifth grade asking my teacher to take me to the hospital. He said he could not take me then, but we could go the following day. And I replied, "I do not think my dad is going to be there tomorrow." But my teacher did not understand. So, in fifth grade, I took it upon myself to go independently. I was determined to see my dad. I felt something was wrong, and I needed to see him urgently. So yes, you guessed it, I went to the hospital by myself. When I arrived at the hospital, I was stopped by a guard. He said I was too young to go in. When the guard turned his head, I dashed up the back stairs. But lo and behold, the guard had grabbed my arm. In the blink of an eye, I realized we were standing right outside of my dad's hospital room. Some of my family and elders from the church were there, and they told the guard it was ok for me to see my dad.

James 4:13-15 NIV, "Now listen, you who say, "Today or tomorrow we will go to this or that city, spend a year there, carry on business and make money." Why you do not even know what will happen tomorrow. What is your life? You are a mist that appears for a little while and then vanishes. Instead, you ought to say, "If it is the Lord's will, we will live and do this or that."

I will never forget when I walked in and saw my dad and the elders were singing the hymn hold to God's unchanging hands. I cried bitterly. That evening my dad passed. And I remember telling my teacher the next day that my dad did not make it. I remembered that the day before my teacher said it would be ok, your dad will be there tomorrow. That was one of the saddest days of my life. Because I felt like a part of me was gone. I could not imagine not having a dad in my life, even though I am from a family of twelve, and I have nine sisters and two brothers. But it was the plan of God for my life.

One of the ways we can live a life as an overcomer is to depend on the work of the Holy Spirit in us.

1. The Holy Spirit indwells believers.
   - ***1st Corinthians 6:19-20 NIV,*** "Do you not know that your bodies are temples of the Holy Spirit, who is in you, whom you have received from God? You are not your own; you were bought at a price. Therefore, honor God with your bodies."

2. The Holy Spirit fills believers.
   - ***Ephesians 5:18 NIV,*** "Do not get drunk on wine, which leads to debauchery. Instead, be filled with the Spirit,"

3. The Holy Spirit produces fruit in the life of believers.
   - Galatians 5:22-23 NIV, "But the fruit of the Spirit is love, joy, peace, forbearance, kindness, goodness, faithfulness, gentleness, and self-control. Against such things, there is no law."

4. The Holy Spirit imparts gifts to believers.
   - ***Romans 12:6-8 NIV,*** "We have different gifts, according to the grace given to each of us. If your gift is prophesying, then prophesy in accordance with your faith; if it is serving, then serve; if it is teaching, then teach; if it is to encourage, then give encouragement; if it is giving, then give generously; if it is to lead, do it diligently; if it is to show mercy, do it cheerfully.

   - ***1st Corinthians. 12:4-11 NIV,*** "There are different kinds of gifts, but the same Spirit distributes them. There are different kinds of service, but the same Lord. There are different kinds of working, but in all of them and in everyone, it is the same God at work. Now to each one the manifestation of the Spirit is given for the common good. To one there is given through the Spirit a message of wisdom, to another a message of knowledge by means of the same Spirit, to another faith by the same Spirit, to another gifts of healing by that one Spirit, to another miraculous powers, to another prophecy, to another distinguishing between spirits, to another speaking in different kinds of tongues, and to still another the interpretation of tongues. All these are the work of one and the same Spirit, and he distributes them to each one, just as he determines."

- *Ephesians 4:4-11 NIV,* "There is one body and one Spirit, just as you were called to one hope when you were called; one Lord, one faith, one baptism; one God and Father of all, who is over all and through all and in all. But to each one of us grace has been given as Christ apportioned it. This is why it says: "When he ascended on high, he took many captives and gave gifts to his people." (What does "he ascended" mean except that he also descended to the lower, earthly regions]? He who descended is the very one who ascended higher than all the heavens, in order to fill the whole universe.) So Christ himself gave the apostles, the prophets, the evangelists, the pastors and teachers,"

5. The Holy Spirit empowers believers.
    - *Acts 1:4-8 NIV,* "On one occasion, while he was eating with them, he gave them this command: "Do not leave Jerusalem, but wait for the gift my Father promised, which you have heard me speak about. For John baptized with water, but in a few days you will be baptized with the Holy Spirit. Then they gathered around him and asked him, "Lord, are you at this time going to restore the kingdom to Israel?" He said to them: "It is not for you to know the times or dates the Father has set by his own authority. But you will receive power when the Holy Spirit comes on you; and you will be my witnesses in Jerusalem, and in all Judea and Samaria, and to the ends of the earth."

I still look back on my youth with great fondness. Enjoying Sunday school, learning the Word, hearing the stories, and my favorite, having a contest for quoting the most scriptures. We won gifts in Sunday School. What a great time of life. As I got a little older, I would ride on the church van to help keep the kids quiet. As I look back, I can see that I was always busy for the Kingdom. And I felt respected as a kid because the other kids would say, "Here comes preacher boy," but it was in a kind, respectful way.

My pastor, Reverend Thea F. Jones, said, "Every great thing that God gives to man, in order to be enjoyed, must be shared. Love is one of our greatest gifts from heaven, but love can only bring fulfillment when shared with someone else."

Mark Hatcher, Sr.

Chapter 5

Prayer Life:
Prayer, Prayer, &
More Prayer

Of all the things Christ wants for us, loving him and focusing our attention on him are the most important. ~ Charles Stanley

The deepest parts of my life and ministry come from having a strong prayer life. I grew up in a spiritual and loving home where my parents were prayer warriors. My mother is 93 now, with a sharp memory – she is a big supporter and encourager. Seeing her pray is what made me see the profound value of prayer. Everyone does not pray in the same way; we are each unique. We each have our own relationship with God and our own way that we encounter God. I like to kneel and pray; you may stand and wave your hands. But what I know for sure is that prayer is the one power on earth that orders the power of heaven. The way I see it is, "No prayer, no power."

Matthew 6:9-10 NIV
The Lord's Prayer

"This, then, is how you should pray: "Our Father in heaven, hallowed be your name, your kingdom come, your will be done, on earth as it is in heaven.

Mark 11:24 NIV

Therefore, I tell you, whatever you ask for in prayer, believe that you have received it, and it will be yours.

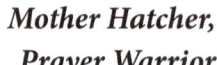

Mother Hatcher,
Prayer Warrior

Prayer is one of the most amazing opportunities because it lifts us into the presence of the Almighty God. If we calm our hearts in God's presence and if we can listen for His voice, we will be transported into a divine conversation, and yes, you will find yourself sharing your deepest heartfelt thoughts and prayers while receiving God's revelation that will build your spirit and guide you on your day-to-day journey.

- ❖ Be sure to remember God and thank Him for your answered prayers.
- ❖ Be sure to ask God for His will in your life.
- ❖ Feel free to let God know what you need. You have not because you ask not.
- ❖ Check your heart and ask for forgiveness.
- ❖ Pray in agreement with a trusted friend.
- ❖ The Word of God is powerful. Pray the scriptures.
- ❖ We have authority in Christ, memorize scripture.

PRAY WITHOUT CEASING

I was chosen for the challenge because I had a real strong prayer life, and when we look at the life of Jesus, no matter how God used him, he always took time to talk to God. If Jesus could take time out of his schedule for God, we have no excuse.

Another way I know I was chosen for the challenge is because my faith in God is extraordinarily powerful. I do not just operate in the typical type of faith, but God has blessed me with the gift of faith. The gift of faith is when whatever you read or whatever God says, that settles it in your mind. You do not even waiver in your heart. You believe God totally, no matter what it is. God gave me that kind of faith because it would take that kind of faith to withstand the challenges I experienced with the hurt and demands of life. I could not waver in my faith because of the assignment and call to restore this old waste space. It is a historical landmark space. And it has touched many, many, many lives.

I have seen the multitudes healed and delivered. I have seen the power of God. I have seen people who were crippled get out of their wheelchair healed. I have seen deaf ears that were stopped, opened, and right in front of me. I saw a woman who looked eight months pregnant because of a tumor in her stomach get prayed for and then fall under the spiritual power, and she got up. That is why I call this place a miracle on Broad Street.

- ❖ "For his anger lasts only a moment, but his <u>favor</u> lasts a lifetime. Weeping may last for the night, but joy comes with the morning." Psalm 30:5 NLT

- ❖ "But Noah found <u>favor</u> with the Lord." Genesis 6:8 NLT

- ❖ "May the <u>favor</u> of the Lord our God on us; establish the work of our hands upon us- yes, establish the work of our hands!" Psalm 90:17 NIV

- ❖ "For the Lord God is a sun and shield; the Lord bestows <u>favor</u> and honor. No good thing does he withhold from those whose walk blamelessly." Psalm 84:11 NIV

- ❖ The Spirit of the Lord is upon me, because the Lord has anointed me to proclaim good news to the poor. He has sent me to bind up the brokenhearted, to proclaim freedom for the captives and release from darkness for the prisoners, to proclaim the year of the Lord's <u>favor</u> and the day of vengeance of our God, to comfort all who mourn," Isaiah 61:1-2 NIV

> Declare favor over your life. Nothing happens until you speak it into existence.

Chapter 4

The Road:
When the Road is Rough
& the Going Gets Tough

Learn to worship God as the God who does wonders, who wishes to prove in you that he can do something supernatural and divine. ~ Andrew Murray

What do you do when you have nothing? When I was starting out, that's pretty much how things were. Of course, some scoffed at me, laughed at me, and had negative opinions of me. Have you ever been in a place like that where you had no one who shared your vision? And even my loved ones were sick and tired of me putting personal finances toward the ministry.

To say I went through a rough patch would be an understatement. But God directed me to a group of local pastors who gave me their used Sunday school books so I could at least have a start. I was grateful, to say the least.

A song says, "The road is rough, and the going gets tough, and the hills are hard to climb. I started a long time ago, and there is no doubt in my mind, I've decided to make Jesus my choice."

Here are a few things to think about when you find yourself on a winding road.

- ❖ Many people use a GPS tracker to get somewhere they are not entirely familiar with.

- ❖ Personal road mapping is an excellent idea to keep you on your road to calling and purpose.

- ❖ Pause and think about the road ahead of you and how you will take time to prepare for your God-given journey.

- ❖ Now is not the time to walk aimlessly. It is the time to be alert and on board with the call of God.

- ❖ Ask yourself what your goals are for the next week, the next day, or the next opportunity.

- ❖ Write down some goals that will help you get there.

- ❖ It is time to make a framework for your success.

Praise be to God! In 1983 I was able to launch the Mark Hatcher Evangelistic Association. Sunday, October 2, 1983, at 7:00 pm began my ministry. Our congregation was able to cobble some things together and find a diamond in the rough, yes, pretty much a dump yard, but to me, it was a diamond. Yes, it needed a lot of work, but since there were construction workers, architects, electricians, plumbers, etc., we had willing laborers. We got it for a steal of a deal, and boom, our church ministry was back in growth mode.

But just when things seemed to be going well, my pastor Rev. Thea Jones died. I was devastated, but God held me close and helped me continue the legacy of my former Shepherd. My mind wandered back to the prophecy he gave me as a child. He foretold of me pastoring a large church, not fully visualizing that the large church was his church where miracles, healings, and deliverance had taken place. It was time to step into his mantle.

~ ~ ~

In 1995, I co-sponsored a convention at the old Philadelphia Civic Center with Dr. Morris Cerullo and Bishop T.D. Jakes as keynote speakers. While he was in prayer in his hotel, Dr. Cerullo and Mama Cerullo delivered a word to me saying, "God is going to give you the city." God used Bishop Jakes to declare personal elevation in the Kingdom of God. I wrestled with the prophecy spoken by Bishop Jakes until it became clear to me what God was doing. I experienced a flashback of my childhood days growing up in the Met. In the spirit, God took me through the entire building. I saw room after room, stairwell after stairwell, closets, bathrooms, floor after floor. I knew every inch of my former church from the many years of attending, worshiping, and working there.

When I talked to Helen Jones, the widow of Rev. Thea Jones, the next day, she explained that the building was in danger of being demolished, and she asked me to come to court with her the next day. When the judge asked me how much money I had, I told him I had just come here to inquire. I was upfront and told him I had zero dollars. He calmly told me $600,000 to stabilize the building, and if I'm interested, I only had 30 days to stabilize the building. And he was sure to mention that if L & I were not satisfied, the building would be torn down.

Here is what I believe. I believe God is a God of timing. Coming to the court that day allowed us the opportunity to stay at the hand of the wrecking ball. God gave me the vision to restore the desolate structure. We immediately went to work filling in the cracks, removing fallen plaster and weed trees from the façade, cinder blocking the window and the door openings with a tiny work crew that God provided by donations, contributions, and volunteers.

One thing I know for sure: God is never early, and He is never late, but he is always right on time.

"In you, Lord, I have taken refuge; let me never be put to shame; deliver me in your righteousness. Turn your ear to me, come quickly to my rescue; be my rock of refuge, a strong fortress to save me." ~Psalms 31:1-2

During November 1995, Holy Ghost Headquarters marched around the walls of the former Metropolitan Opera House in faith to claim the place where the divine presence of angels was ushered in by the former fervent worship of believers. We acquired the necessary permits, blocked off the street, and marched around the building seven times. After the shouts of praise, we rolled into another rough patch of the journey.

What should have been a time of thanksgiving for saving the building changed into a time of trials. The pressure of the monumental task to keep things moving with the building was outrageous. Problems within the building were being discovered, which required more money. During its demise, a water main had broken, and there were four feet of standing water against the foundation.

My children were growing up, and my family's dynamics were changing. Tensions were at an all-time high, and the only thing I could do was to walk humbly before the Lord and seek wisdom.

We wrote letters asking for donations and contributions. Pastors that had come out of the Met and established churches and pastors I knew personally did not even bother to respond. But one thing I knew for sure, I could not come down off the wall, as the entire city was waiting to see us fail. Public opinions evoked slanderous comments about our mission. The owner changed up on us and became very vindictive. We were put out of the building once again.

But wait, there is more. In 1996, Holy Ghost Headquarters received the option to buy the building for $500,000, but only if we could stabilize it within thirty days. Well, guess what, we did. Plus, a State Senator and a State Representative put in $500,000 each using state redevelopment grants. This God story has twists and turns that just keep bringing us to the next right thing.

By 1998, church membership began to decline, and the negative news about our situation reached the ears of Dr. Cerullo. He became instrumental and influential in assisting us with the procurement of our facility. With the help of Dr. Cerullo, we purchased Holy Ghost Headquarters Revival Center. HGH purchased the building from the Thea Jones Evangelistic Association. That meant that we could buy brand new carpet, chairs, curtains, a state-of-the-art sound system, and all we needed in the main auditorium to transform it into a beautiful sanctuary.

Some of the older renderings of the MET.

If you notice, this one still has the awning at the corner of Broad & Poplar.

This is the more modern era of the MET (70's)

After many years of decay, this incredible landmark was refurbished. This space is on the main floor of the old Opera House, now called the MET.

Chapter 5

Camp Meetings

Learn to worship God as the God who does wonders, who wishes to prove in you that he can do something supernatural and divine. ~ Andrew Murray

At Holy Ghost Headquarters at the Met, a significant aspect of the church's life is the Camp Meetings. If you have not been to a camp meeting, you are missing out on one of the most vibrant aspects of the church.

Camp Meetings can be outdoors or indoors. Camp Meeting can run day and night. It all depends upon the groups that gather to it. This one thing I know for sure is that when Camp Meeting arrives, you will never be the same again. It is preaching, prayer, singing, and possibly baptisms. However, God leads. This phenomenon is a fantastic opportunity for all people of all ages to gather in a meeting to release and express our love for God or to seek God and hear God.

Camp meetings go way back to the frontier times to now. The people were living so far apart during those times that they needed to find a way of building community. They decided to use revivals as a great way to gather. The camp-meeting movement influenced many people in the Appalachian religion. The people who came to these meetings camped outside or pitched a tent to stay overnight. I am sure some people just came because they were curious, but that is good. In doing so, they may find something they genuinely need. Great things happen at the camp meetings.

Holy Ghost Headquarters at the Met is an evangelistic church that welcomes participation from all Christian denominations. There are no registration fees. God gave me the call to host annual camp meetings with worship services so high in the spirit that would cause you to come out and feast on the glory of God with all the handclapping, foot-stomping, tongue-speaking, being slain in the spirit, shouting and dancing. Yes, all of that. Why? Because spiritual revitalization and renewal hold so much value for our mind, body, and spirit. And connecting to the body of believers in this context is a compelling way to help others advance in their personal and spiritual life.

2 Days OF HOLYGHOST POWER

EVANGELIST RUBY HOLLAND-HUTCHINS

CAMPMEETING
NOTHING LACKING

CHIEF APOSTLE MARK A. HATCHER

HOLYGHOST HEADQUARTERS
REVIVAL CENTER AT THE MET
858 North Broad St.
Philidelphia, PA 19130
SERVICE TIME.:.:7PM

AUG 25-26 2013

SUN .::6PM
MON .::7PM

Chapter 6

Life is a Journey

"God never said that the journey would be easy, but He did say that the arrival would be worthwhile" - Max Lucado

The great thing about HGH Revival Center at the MET is that we are a small group in a prominent location. Our congregation is set in grand surroundings that may take your breath away. But we are indeed a family. We have a big heart for the community, and we believe in meeting needs spiritually and physically. In our services, you will see well-to-do people who have challenges and struggle just like anyone else. As a body, we see ourselves as our brother's and our sister's keeper.

One of the things we pride ourselves on is that in all of the building and work that was needed to restore our establishment, we never relied on the government. All odds were against us, and yes, we had significant challenges, but we operated from the sixth sense, the power of God. And I must admit it was like we had a deep inner drive coupled with a deep inner peace that drew us to our goal.

In the early days, some people had a negative perspective of our ministry, but as with anything, time tends to change things. We grow with time, knowledge, wisdom. Moreover, time makes things better.

In all churches, members sometimes attend for a season, and members leave. I have realized that their departure may not be due to anything negative. God has a timing for everything. I have seen members return to the ministry after some time. Some just needed a break to care for loved ones, and it had nothing to do with the church. Others may not have the same object as some when attending the ministry. I also realize that people have a lot to deal with outside the church- for example, family, work, and other opportunities. I honor that.

Within the church or outside the church in the community, I am always concerned about the well-being of our members and friends, and that includes inviting whosoever will. No one person is different from the other. We are one. No matter how large the church becomes, I hope always to find ways to provide a sense of blessed connectedness.

How Did You Meet Pastor Mark Hatcher?
Name: Thomas Logan

I met Mark Hatcher 35 years ago. We lived near each other, and we both had children of the same age. I saw that Mark was starting a church and so I placed my children in the Sunday school. It was a great connection; I knew some of his family from the neighborhood, and our friendship grew.

I attended his first church on Glenwood Avenue, then the location Thea Jones utilized, and finally The MET until this very day. I ended up working with him for twenty-five or more years. I was maintaining and keeping the building. One of the things I realized early on was that people wanted to destroy Mark's dream. They tried to tear the building down. But it was a vital part of the area, and I wanted to make sure it stayed in Pastor Mark's hands. I was also knowledgeable of the political side of things. Therefore, I kept an eye out for dangers seen and unseen in that arena. It was a crazy ride with the city pushing to get rid of this remarkable landmark. I am glad it did not work, and now we have a building we can be proud of today.

How Did You Meet Pastor Mark Hatcher?
Name: Gwendolyn Winfrey

I met Mark Hatcher in 1996. We connected when he requested that I help him set up a non-profit organization. He was very engaged with moving things forward, but with the breadth of renovation the MET needed to rise fully, it required other hands and feet. With the legal background and knowledge of critical aspects of nonprofit standards, I realized I was the person to jump in. At that time, Mark was also serving the community in many valuable ways, and my input could be a great way to assist this significant endeavor.

Watching the play-by-play segments of Mark Hatcher's journey and how he was raised in that church and in that community and continues to serve faithfully in season and out of season means a lot. It's like a vision is being fulfilled for God's purpose.

Chapter 7

Renovated Met

NORTH PHILADELPHIA COMMUNITY DEVELOPMENT CORPORATION AT THE MET

One of the great things that happened in 1998 is that North Philadelphia Community Development Corporation at the MET was established. It provides community development services and programs in the North Central area of Philadelphia and the greater Philadelphia community. Since its organization, all of the development corporation's energies have been devoted to the completion.

Phase 1 renovations included stabilization and renovation of exterior brickwork, replacement of entrance doors at the main entrance on Poplar Street, replacement of basic systems (including a basement pump).

Phase 2 included a complete renovation of the auditorium on the 1st and 2nd-floor levels; Renovation of office spaces and conference rooms on the first and second floor levels; Additional exterior brick work and installation of doors and windows (Poplar Street); and Installation of an HVAC system.

Phase 3 included renovation of the third-floor level of the auditorium, the third-floor ceiling and ceiling over the stage area, renovation of five Broad Street facing storefronts (to house small businesses and one historic exhibit center as The Avenue of the Arts North Retail Gallery, completion of the exterior brickwork (Broad Street, Carlisle Street) and installation of a commercial kitchen. These final phase renovations were followed by a historic restoration campaign designed to restore the architectural gem to its original grandeur.

The Executive Director of the corporation and a team of volunteers have conducted community surveys in selected segments of the target service area and have determined program priorities as:

- Crime Reduction Programs
- Youth Service Programs After-School, Summer, etc.
- Job Development services

As a result of this community input, many non-profit services and programs were planned to include an ex-offender re-entry program, a computer technology center, a career preparation training center, and children and family services programs. The board of directors is completing a strategic plan to prioritize attention to these areas in the development of services to the community.

Beautiful Views at the Renovated MET

The Auditorium

Side Entrance

Grande Salle

2nd Level

$100,000 Square Foot Theater!

Chapter 8

Blast From the Past

Amazing Worship & Events at the MET

Let the Glory of the Lord, Rise Among Us

Let the Praises of our King Rise Among Us

Blast From the Glorious Past!

2001 Hosted Apostle Richard D. Henton

2003 Camp Meeting: The Last Outpouring

2004 Camp Meeting: 20 Days of Meeting

2005 Camp Meeting: 20 Days of Meeting

2005 Fall Revival: Dr. Morris Cerullo

2006 Youth Explosion: Ty Tribbett

2007 Camp Meeting: Alvin Slaughter

2007 Steering Committee: Citywide Crusade

2008 Camp Meeting: Rev. Dr. Patricia Phillips

2009 Camp Meeting: Evangelist R. W. Schambach

2010 Camp Meeting: 20 Days of Meeting

2011 Seven Night Encounter: Dr. Juanita Bynum

2012 Camp Meeting & 30 Years of Ministry

2014 Camp Meeting: The Greater & the Major

2018 Pre-New Year's Eve: Dr. Cindy Trimm

2019 He's Alive Meets the MET

2019 One Night Only w/Bishop Marvin Sapp

2004

Pastor
Jackie McCoullough

Apostle
Richard D. Henton

Bishop Van Dash

Pastor
Rosie Wallace Brown

Pastor
Wynell Freeman

Pastor
Chuck Lawrence

Pastor
Thelma Malone

Pastor
Wesley Pinnock

Pastor
William B. Moore

Dr. Wilson Goode

Pastor
Clement M. Lupton, III

Apostle Kenneth Porter

Bishop Iona E. Locke

Evg. Alice Martin

Rev. Louise Wms-Bishop

Dr. Morris Cerullo

Evg. Ann Davis

Bishop Charles E. Wms

Camp Meeting 2010 Sunday May 23 - Friday June 11

Apostle
Wyvell Freeman
Sun May 23 @ 6:30 PM

Pastor
Sheryl Brady
Mon May 24 @ 7:30 PM

Pastor
Jackie McCullough
Tue May 25
Wed May 26 @ 7:30 PM

Bishop
Noel Jones
Thurs May 27 @ 7:30 PM

Bishop
Ralph "Donnie" Graves
Fri May 28 @ 7:30 PM

Keith & Karl Edmonds
K&K Mime
YOUTH EXPLOSION
Sat May 29 @ 6:30 PM

Evangelist
Larry Stacy
Sun May 30 @ 11:00 AM

Dr. Marvin L. Sapp
Sun May 30 @ 7:00 PM

Minister
Alvin Slaughter
Mon May 31 @ 6:30 PM

Dr. Rance Allen
Tues Jun 1 2010 @ 7:30

Pastor
Paula White
Wed Jun 2 @ 7:30 PM

Dr. Jamal Harrison-Bryant
Thurs Jun 3 @ 7:30 PM

Prophetess
Juanita Bynum II
Fri Jun 4 @ 7:30 PM
Sat Jun 5 @ 6:30 PM

Reverend
Louise Williams-Bishop
Sun Jun 7 @ 11:00 AM

Prophet
Todd Hall
Sun Jun 6 @ 6:30 PM
Mon Jun 7 @ 7:30 PM

Pastor
Ray Benard
Tue Jun 8 @ 7:30 PM

Bishop
Darrell Hines
Wed Jun 9 @ 7:30 PM

Apostle
Richard D. Henton
Thurs Jun 10 @ 7:30 PM
Fri Jun 11 @ 7:30 PM

Chapter 9

Great Memories

Ordination as Apostle

Laying On of Hands & Prophesying

A Table Set for a King! Happy Birthday Apostle!

Chapter 10

Ribbon Cutting

Ribbon Cutting! Mayor Kenny, Darrell Clarke, Patty Jackson, Eric Blumenfeld, & Mark Hatcher Sr.

Live Nation Regional President, Geoff Gordon

Developer Eric Blumenfeld speaks at the ribbon cutting.

Chapter 11

MET Photos and News Clips

**Interior of The Met Philadelphia
(CONTRIBUTED PHOTOS courtesy of Live)**

Once a grande dame on North Broad, the Metropolitan Opera House now houses a church. The state is offering some help.

The Rev. Mark Hatcher stands in the renovated worship area of Holy Ghost Headquarters. The church uses two floors of the former opera house that it bought in 1996. Top, old chairs sit on the balcony.

Salvation and preservation

By Mitch Lipka
INQUIRER STAFF WRITER

The view from North Broad Street of the once-grand Metropolitan Opera House is not pretty.

There is barely a hint of the glory days of the building or its surroundings. Boards cover windows, concrete is crumbling, and trees are growing through bricks and mortar on upper floors that sadly overlook the hulk of a onetime Burger King.

Yet the tale of the former opera house is not one of woe, but of hope, determination and faith.

A decade ago, the building at 858 N. Broad St. was facing the wrecking ball. Its state of disrepair inside and out was so great that the city deemed it a hazard.

Somehow, that did not deter the Rev. Mark Hatcher, but rather instilled in him a fierce determination to keep the building from being destroyed and restore it to its former glory.

"One night I went to sleep,
See **OPERA HOUSE** on B4

The building for years sat in disrepair. The state grants totaling $1 million will go toward rehabilitating the Broad Street facade and putting in four or five storefronts.

To see more photos of the Metropolitan Opera House, go to **http://go.philly.com/met**

By Kristin E. Holmes
Staff Writer

On December 9, six days after 3,500 devoted attendees of Bob Dylan pack the grandly renovated Met Philadelphia, another audience, one carrying Bibles and Holy oil, will gather in the North Broad Street concert venue to worship an even high power. The congregation of Holy Ghost Headquarters will be returning for its first Sunday service in the refurbished building – a historic former opera house that had been church-owned for 60 years. Members had saved the 39,000 square foot structure from demolition and labored to maintain it, only to have the burden grow too onerous for the Pentecostal flock of a few hundred.

So, in 2012, Holy Ghost Headquarters sold a 50 percent stake in the property to Eric Blumenthal for $1, a share in rental profits, and the right to continue worshipping there. The deal opened the way for a $56 million makeover of the Metropolitan Opera House.

HOLY SPACES

KEEPING THE FAITH

Congregations sell off properties but retain a place to worship.

By Kristin E. Holmes
STAFF WRITER

On Dec. 9, six days after 3,500 devotees of Bob Dylan pack the grandly renovated Met Philadelphia, another audience, one carrying Bibles and holy oil, will gather in the North Broad Street concert venue to worship an even higher power.

The congregation of Holy Ghost Headquarters will be returning for its first Sunday service in the refurbished building — a historic, former opera house that had been church-owned for 60 years. Members had saved the 39,000-square-foot structure from demolition and labored to maintain it, only to have the burden grow too onerous for the Pentecostal flock of a few hundred.

So, in 2012, Holy Ghost Headquarters sold a 50 percent stake in the property to developer Eric Blumenthal for $1, a share in rental profits, and the right to continue worshiping there. The deal opened the way for a $56 million makeover of the old Metropolitan Opera House, built in 1908 by theater impresario

See **CHURCHES** on A4

> " This whole area has changed. ...
> You can't keep up with changes in your neighborhood with a raggedy building. ... We chose to stay and work it out with a developer.

Mark Hatcher, above, pastor of Holy Ghost Headquarters

Services are held at New Spirit, which sold its church and now shares space. At top, the Met concert venue is taking shape after a church sale.

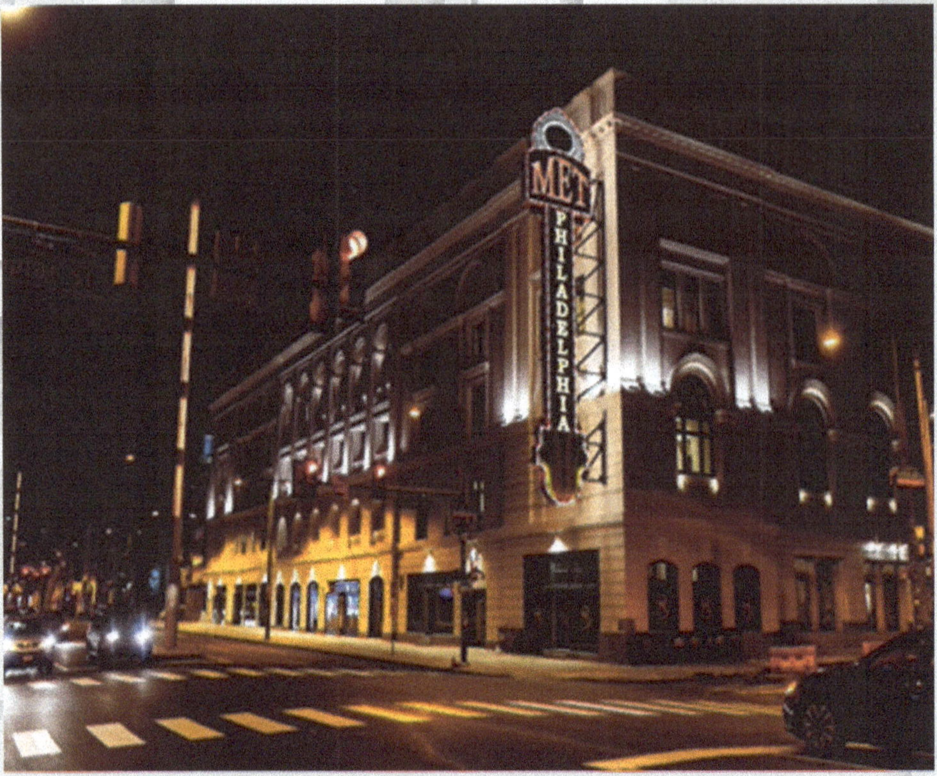
MET
PHILADELPHIA
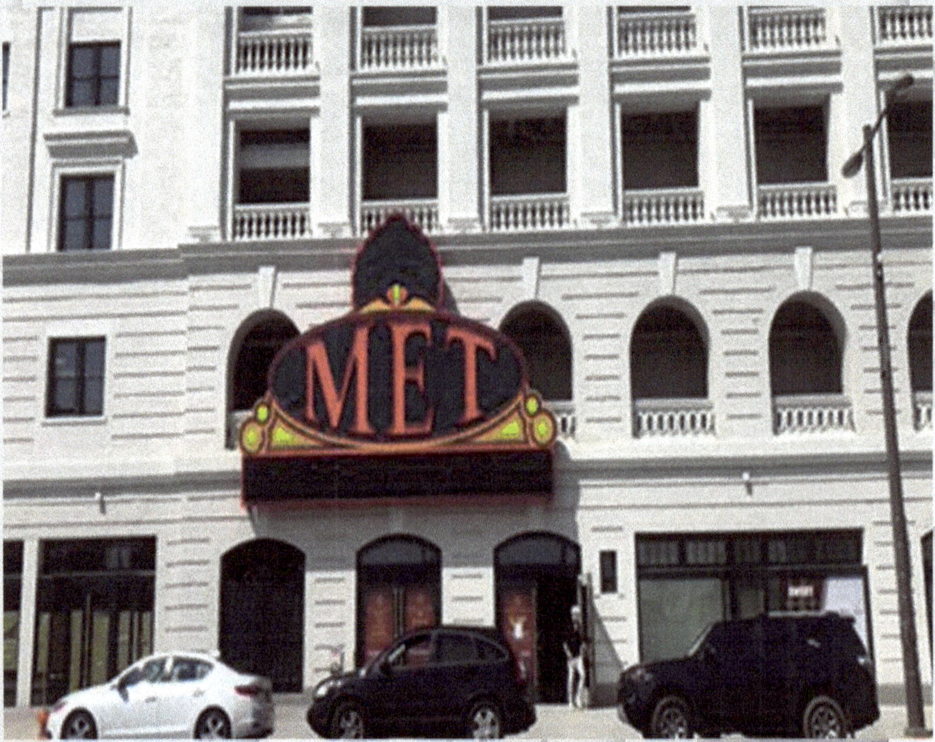
MET

Chapter 12

Ending Segments

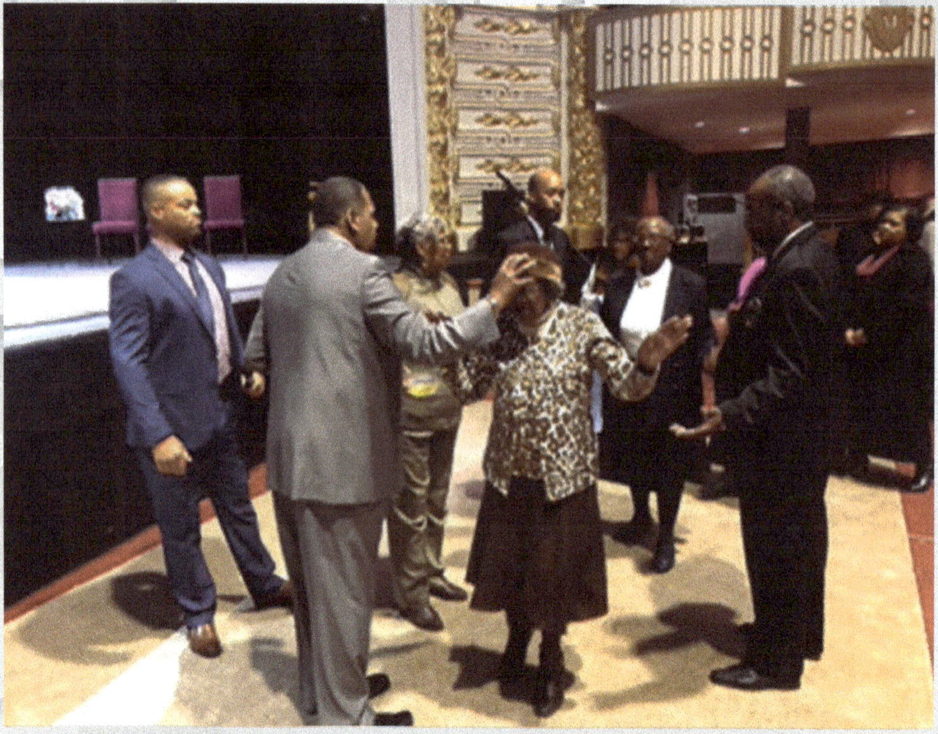

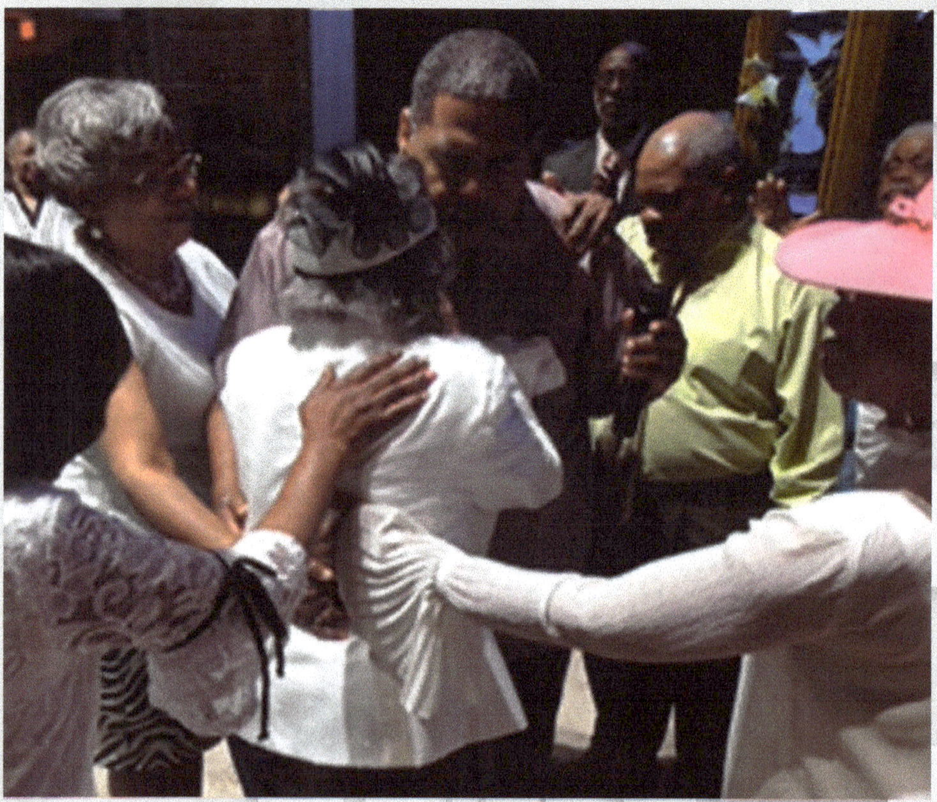

PRAYER TIME

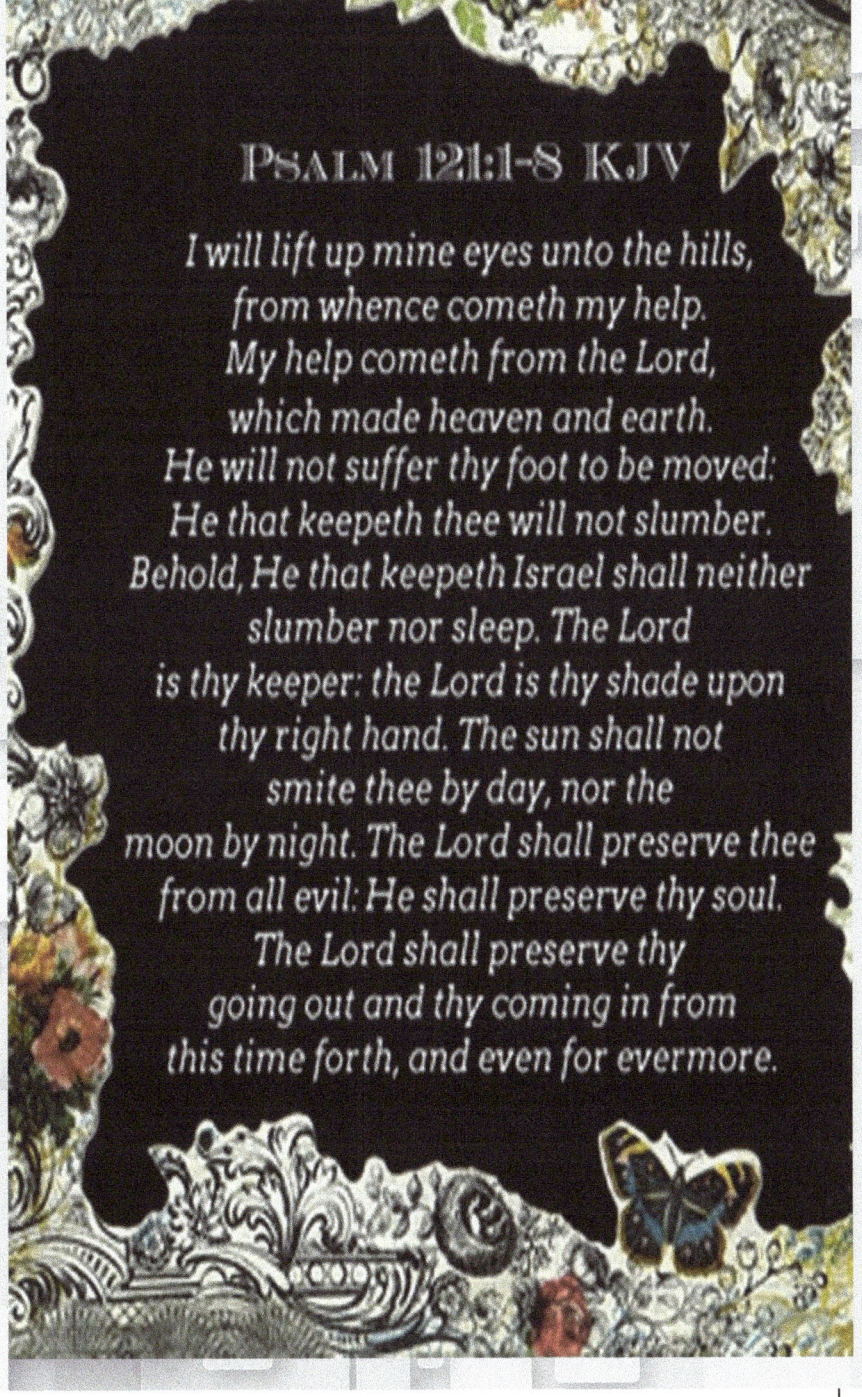

Psalm 121:1-8 KJV

*I will lift up mine eyes unto the hills,
from whence cometh my help.
My help cometh from the Lord,
which made heaven and earth.
He will not suffer thy foot to be moved:
He that keepeth thee will not slumber.
Behold, He that keepeth Israel shall neither
slumber nor sleep. The Lord
is thy keeper: the Lord is thy shade upon
thy right hand. The sun shall not
smite thee by day, nor the
moon by night. The Lord shall preserve thee
from all evil: He shall preserve thy soul.
The Lord shall preserve thy
going out and thy coming in from
this time forth, and even for evermore.*

Many times, people think of leadership as being in charge. I don't see it that way. Being an Apostle is a calling, and it makes you highly humble. Great leaders must be honest and live with integrity. Some people need the ministry of Apostles, Prophets, Evangelists, Pastors & Teachers, and I am grateful to use my gifts to serve whosoever will.

Apostle: The Bible declares that Jesus is the "Apostle and High Priest of our faith." Hebrews 3:1 NIV, "Therefore, holy brothers and sisters, who share in the heavenly calling, fix your thoughts on Jesus, whom we acknowledge as our apostle and high priest."

Prophet: Jesus is the proclaimer of truth, the revelation of the heart of God, and he foretold events that were to come as well.

He is spoken of in Deuteronomy 18:15 NIV, "The Lord your God will raise up for you a prophet like me from among you, from your fellow Israelites. You must listen to him."

Evangelist: Jesus was the greatest proclaimer of the good news that the world has ever known.

"The Spirit of the Sovereign LORD is on me, because the LORD has anointed me to proclaim good news to the poor. He has sent me to bind up the brokenhearted, to proclaim freedom for the captives and release from darkness for the prisoners," Isaiah 61:1 NIV.

Pastor: Jesus said of Himself: "I am the good shepherd. The good shepherd lays down His life for the sheep." John 10:11 NIV.

Teacher: Jesus Christ is the greatest teacher the world has ever known. John 13:13 NIV, "You call Me Teacher and Lord, and rightly so, for that is what I am."

I started writing this book in the midst of the 2020 pandemic, surrounded by the world being in crisis and fear. If you are reading this, it is clear that you have survived much of the tragedy, and for that, I am delighted. Writing a book is not easy. You must go back into your arsenal of life to remember and recollect all of the beautiful encounters you have been a part of and thank God. What an incredible journey! In this book and our connection with each other, I hope you have found:

- Restoration
- Transformation
- Faith, Hope, Peace, Joy

- Confidence
- God's Plan for Your Life
- Power & Glory from on High
- Anointing
- Strength & Motivation
- Encouragement
- Favor
- Blessings
- Surprises
- Purpose
- Laughter
- Rivers of Living Water
- God Ideas

And for the record, don't think I left the building work to everyone else. No, I put my hands and my heart to the plow of this great work because I wanted God to be well pleased.

GRATEFUL AFFIRMATIONS

- We are grateful that God is living on the inside of us.
- We are grateful that love is pouring out of us and into the world.
- We are grateful that our presence is producing excellent results in our community.
- We are grateful that people are being blessed in our midst.
- We are grateful to give God the glory for all He has continued to do.
- We are grateful that we are walking in the purpose of God for our lives.
- We are grateful for ways that have been made for us to carry out our calling.
- We are grateful to flow in courage and strength by Christ Jesus consistently.
- We are grateful that our lives are lining up with God's grand plans for us.
- We are grateful that we are steadily moving forward.
- We are grateful that our lives encourage others to do great things for God.
- We are grateful that we hold every moment sacred in God's plan for us.

CHOOSE CHRIST EVERY DAY

Everything that we experience is about our growth and choosing Christ in it. Every encounter, hardship, celebration, and our very existence is about becoming more than we were. I'm not necessarily referring to more in status, but more in spirit, grace, heart, faith, and love.

Ask yourself if you have been choosing Christ each day. Ask God how you can become more in spirit, greater in grace, tr of heart, stronger in faith, and more expansive in your capacity to love.

After asking, sit with your journal and pen and listen for God's answers. Write what you hear in that innermost part of you knitted together with God.

Choose Christ Every Day.

Welcome To The New Home of
HOLY GHOST HEADQUARTERS
REVIVAL CENTER AT THE MET

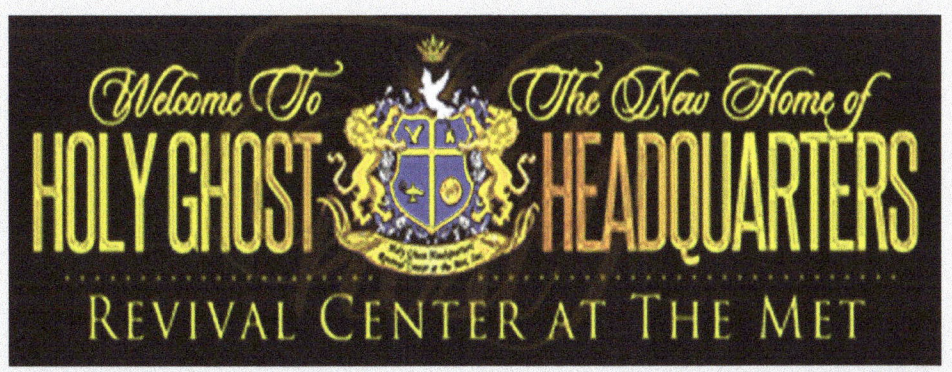

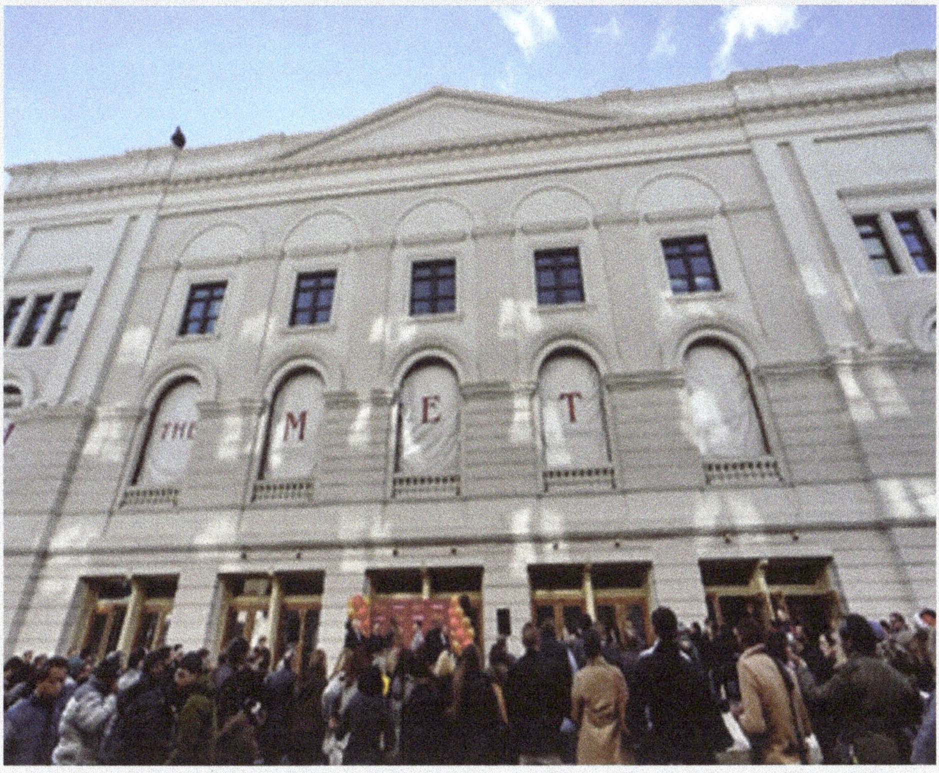

www.ingramcontent.com/pod-product-compliance
Lightning Source LLC
Chambersburg PA
CBHW061204070526
44579CB00010B/121